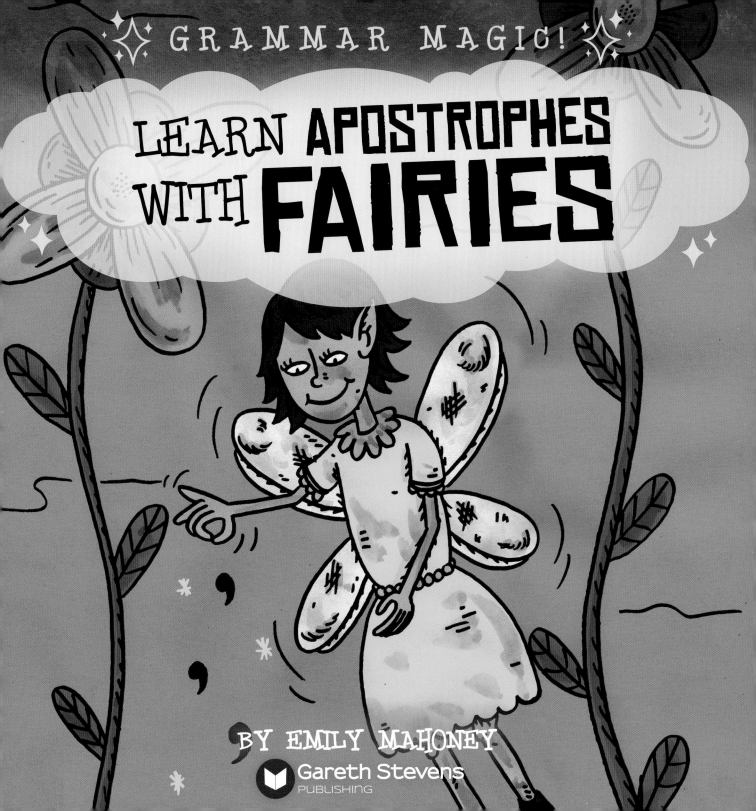

Please visit our website, www.garethstevens.com. For a free color catalog of all our high-quality books, call toll free 1-800-542-2595 or fax 1-877-542-2596.

Library of Congress Cataloging-in-Publication Data

Names: Mahoney, Emily Jankowski, author.
Title: Learn apostrophes with fairies / Emily Mahoney.
Description: New York : Gareth Stevens Publishing, 2021. | Series: Grammar magic! | Includes bibliographical references and index. | Summary: "Apostrophes can be tricky, but the fun fairies in this book will help readers learn how to use them correctly!"-- Provided by publisher.
Identifiers: LCCN 2019027333 | ISBN 9781538247242 | ISBN 9781538247259 (library binding) | ISBN 9781538247235 (paperback) | ISBN 9781538247266 (ebook)
Subjects: LCSH: English language--Punctuation--Juvenile literature. | Apostrophe--Juvenile literature. | Fairies--Juvenile literature.
Classification: LCC PE1450 .M332 2020 | DDC 421--dc23
LC record available at https://lccn.loc.gov/2019027333

First Edition

Published in 2021 by
Gareth Stevens Publishing
111 East 14th Street, Suite 349
New York, NY 10003

Designer: Sarah Liddell
Editor: Kate Mikoley
Illustrator: Bobby Griffiths

Photo credits: Background used throughout solarbird/Shutterstock.com; p. 4 begemot_30/Shutterstock.com; p. 5 Richie Chan/Shutterstock.com; p. 6 pfluegler-photo/Shutterstock.com; p. 8 Natalia Klenova/Shutterstock.com; p. 10 Fer Gregory/Shutterstock.com; pp. 12, 16 Yuganov Konstantin/Shutterstock.com; p. 14 RUKSUTAKARN studio/Shutterstock.com; p. 18 VicW/Shutterstock.com; p. 20 tomertu/Shutterstock.com; p. 21 Elena Schweitzer/Shutterstock.com.

Printed in the United States of America

Some of the images in this book illustrate individuals who are models. The depictions do not imply actual situations or events.

CPSIA compliance information: Batch #CS20GS: For further information contact Gareth Stevens, New York, New York at 1-800-542-2595.

CONTENTS

Fantastic Fairies 4

Awesome Apostrophes 6

Apostrophes and Possession . . .8

Plural Possessives 14

Crazy Contractions 16

Apostrophes and Pixie Dust. .20

Glossary 22

Answer Key 22

For More Information 23

Index 24

Words in the glossary appear in **bold** type
the first time they are used in the text.

FANTASTIC FAIRIES

You may already know that fairies are small and beautiful **mythical** creatures that look like tiny humans with wings. They usually live in forests or gardens. But did you know that fairies are great at **grammar,** especially apostrophes?

The fairies in this book are here to help you learn about apostrophes and how to use them. They have created questions for you to answer based on what you learn from them. Check your answers using the answer key on page 22.

5

AWESOME APOSTROPHES

Apostrophes can be tricky to use, but luckily these fairies like to help! There are a few rules to follow when using apostrophes, but don't worry. If you follow the rules that the fairies teach you, you'll be great at apostrophes in no time!

An apostrophe is the little mark that you see in writing that looks like this: '
What word in the following sentence has an apostrophe in it?

The fairy's wings were beautiful, shiny, and blue.

7

APOSTROPHES AND POSSESSION

Often, apostrophes are used to show **possession.** This means we use apostrophes to show that something belongs to someone. Usually, this can be done by adding an apostrophe and the letter "s" at the end of the word, like this:

The fairy's slippers were very small.

The slippers belong to the fairy, so we use an apostrophe to show that.

What belongs to the fairy queen in the
following sentence?

The fairy queen's castle had 100 different rooms.

If a name ends with an "s," you can still add the apostrophe and an "s" to show possession, like this:

Mr. Jones's class learned about fairies today.

Just like fairies can be **pranksters,** this rule can be tricky. Sometimes you'll see an apostrophe after the "s," but not a second "s." While this isn't wrong, adding the second "s" after the apostrophe is a more common practice.

✧ MAGICAL FACTS! ✧
IT IS BELIEVED THAT FAIRIES CAN DISAPPEAR WHENEVER THEY WANT. WHAT A COOL TRICK!

Can you add an apostrophe and an "s" to show possession in the sentence below?

James homework was to write a story about where fairies come from.

One rule for fairies is that they shouldn't let humans see them too often. There are rules about when apostrophes shouldn't be used, too. For example, apostrophes shouldn't be used to make a **singular** noun **plural**. If there is more than one of something, just add an "s" without the apostrophe, like this:

A fairy is good at blowing away bad dreams.

✧ MAGICAL FACTS! ✧
FAIRIES ARE SAID TO BE ABLE TO WATCH WHAT YOU DREAM AT NIGHT. WHICH IS HOW THEY CAN GET TO KNOW YOU.

True or false: The following sentence needs an apostrophe added to the word "hundreds."

There are hundreds of different kinds of fairies.

PLURAL POSSESSIVES

Sometimes, something might belong to more than one fairy, and in order to **prevent** a fairy fight, it is important to show that both fairies own it. The same is true with humans! If more than one person owns something, add an "s," and then place the apostrophe after the "s," like this:

The girls' costumes made them look just like fairies.

✧ MAGICAL FACTS! ✧
MANY FAIRIES HAVE WANDS, JUST LIKE TINKERBELL FROM THE STORY PETER PAN SOMETIMES USES.

Where should you add an apostrophe to show that the three fairies own the wands?

The three fairies wands were different, but each was beautiful.

CRAZY CONTRACTIONS

Apostrophes are also used to create contractions. Contractions are used when two words are combined to create one word, like this:

do + not = don't

Think of it as a fairy waving their magic wand over two words to make a whole new word! But don't forget to add the apostrophe to show that magic was used!

Can you combine these words to make contractions?
Don't forget the apostrophe!

should + not =

did + not =

have + not =

How do you know where to put the apostrophe when you make a contraction? The apostrophe **replaces** the letter or letters that were removed. These letters are often at the beginning of the second word. Just like a fairy might leave some pixie dust to show that they visited, the apostrophe shows that some letters were removed.

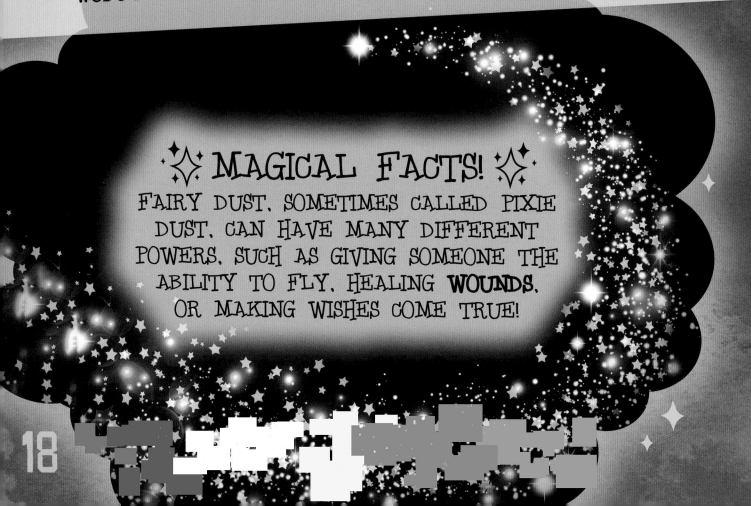

✧ MAGICAL FACTS! ✧
FAIRY DUST, SOMETIMES CALLED PIXIE DUST, CAN HAVE MANY DIFFERENT POWERS, SUCH AS GIVING SOMEONE THE ABILITY TO FLY, HEALING **WOUNDS**, OR MAKING WISHES COME TRUE!

Can you combine these words to make contractions?
Don't forget the apostrophes!

he + will =

I + am =

let + us =

APOSTROPHES AND PIXIE DUST

Apostrophes can be tricky, just like fairies, but you now know that fairies aren't just pranksters that like to play tricks. They're also great at grammar, and can help you to use apostrophes correctly.

Follow the rules to figure out how to use apostrophes correctly. If you get stuck, look at the examples in this book to help you. Maybe if you're lucky, a fairy will wave her wand or sprinkle some pixie dust to help you to put the apostrophe in the right place!

✧ MAGICAL FACTS! ✧
SOME STORIES SAY THAT YOU NEED TO BELIEVE IN FAIRIES TO BE ABLE TO SEE THEM!

21

GLOSSARY

grammar: the rules that show how words are supposed to be used in a language

mythical: existing in your imagination; not real

plural: the form of a word used when talking about more than one thing or person

possession: having or owning something

prankster: someone who likes to play tricks on other people

prevent: to stop something from happening

replace: to use something instead of something else

singular: the form of a word used when talking about only one thing or person

wound: an injury, like a cut or scrape

ANSWER KEY

p. 7: fairy's

p. 9: the castle

p. 11: James's

p. 13: false

p. 15: fairies'

p. 17: shouldn't, didn't, haven't

p. 19: he'll, I'm, let's

FOR MORE INFORMATION

BOOKS

Dignen, Sheila. *Visual Guide to Grammar and Punctuation.* New York, NY: DK Publishing, 2017.

Fiedler, Heidi. *The Know-Nonsense Guide to Grammar.* Lake Forest, CA: Walter Foster Jr., 2017.

Riggs, Kate. *Quotation Marks and Apostrophes.* Mankato, MN: Creative Education, 2017.

WEBSITES

Rules for Finding and Fixing Apostrophe Errors
www.chompchomp.com/rules/aposrules.htm
This page has a helpful list of rules for apostrophe use.

When to Use Apostrophes
ed.ted.com/lessons/when-to-use-apostrophes-laura-mcclure
This informative video shows when to use apostrophes.

INDEX

contractions 16, 17, 18, 19

dream 12

fairy dust 18

forest 4

garden 4

grammar 4, 20

magic 16

mythical 4

noun 12

Peter Pan 14

pixie dust 18, 20

plural 12, 14

possession 8, 10, 11

prankster 10, 20

rules 6, 10, 12, 20

singular 12

Tinkerbell 14

trick 10, 20

wand 14, 15, 16, 20

wings 4